Bubbles and Butterflies

A Calming Coloring Book

for Young Children

By

Sue and Chelsea Badeau

BUBBLES
and
BUTTERFLIES

A CALMING
COLORING BOOK

Sue Badeau   Chelsea Badeau

Introduction: How to Use This Coloring Book

Welcome to "Bubbles & Butterflies," a special calming coloring book designed to support healing and emotional regulation especially for young children (ages two to six) who have experienced trauma, loss or grief. It is intended as a companion to "Building Bridges of Hope: A Coloring Book for Adults Caring for Children Who Have Experienced Trauma," but can also work as a stand-alone resource for children. A third volume, "I'm In Charge of My Feelings!" is available for children aged six through 12.

Within these pages, you will find whimsical, calming and inspiring artwork. The brief text pages, facing each of the art pages, provide easy-to-remember ideas to help children learn to maintain or regain a sense of calm, even when distressed or facing a trauma trigger. The adult version of the book, "Building Bridges of Hope," provides more detail and background information about each of these strategies, tips and tools. Together, these books offer concrete resources for adults and children as they journey from the pain, confusion and stress often associated with trauma to the hope and well-being associated with healing.

The content of the adult version and this companion edition for young children is condensed from the nationally-regarded training on trauma-informed care that author Sue Badeau has shared with thousands of participants in all 50 states. Drawing from her academic background in child development, professional experiences in the child welfare and juvenile justice systems and personal experience raising 22 children, many of whom experienced significant early life trauma, Sue offers a unique combination of clinical and research-based expertise with practical, down-to-earth approaches that busy parents, caregivers, social workers, teachers and therapists can implement with minimal investment of time and money. The strategies and activities have been tried and tested by parents, caregivers and professionals from diverse backgrounds and all walks of life. Additional resources can be found at the end of the book.

The simple artwork has been designed to seed and inspire the child's own creativity. A few blank pages have also been included to allow children to draw their own images. Pulling together her own unique designs with artwork created by several of her siblings and nieces, artist Chelsea Badeau draws on her professional background in the communications arena and years of community service with children to create a unified collection of healing images.

We hope you and the children you love will find hours of joyful and peaceful self-expression while also gaining valuable tools to support growth and healing. Enjoy!

"Faith is taking the first step even when you don't see the whole staircase."
Martin Luther King, Jr.

Sometimes I Am
Scared,
Confused
Lonely or Sad

But Just Like
the Elephant

I Can Be

STRONG

&

BRAVE

When I Am Sad

or Mad

Sometimes I Act

BAD

That's When I Blow

BUBBLES

To Get CALM

& GLAD

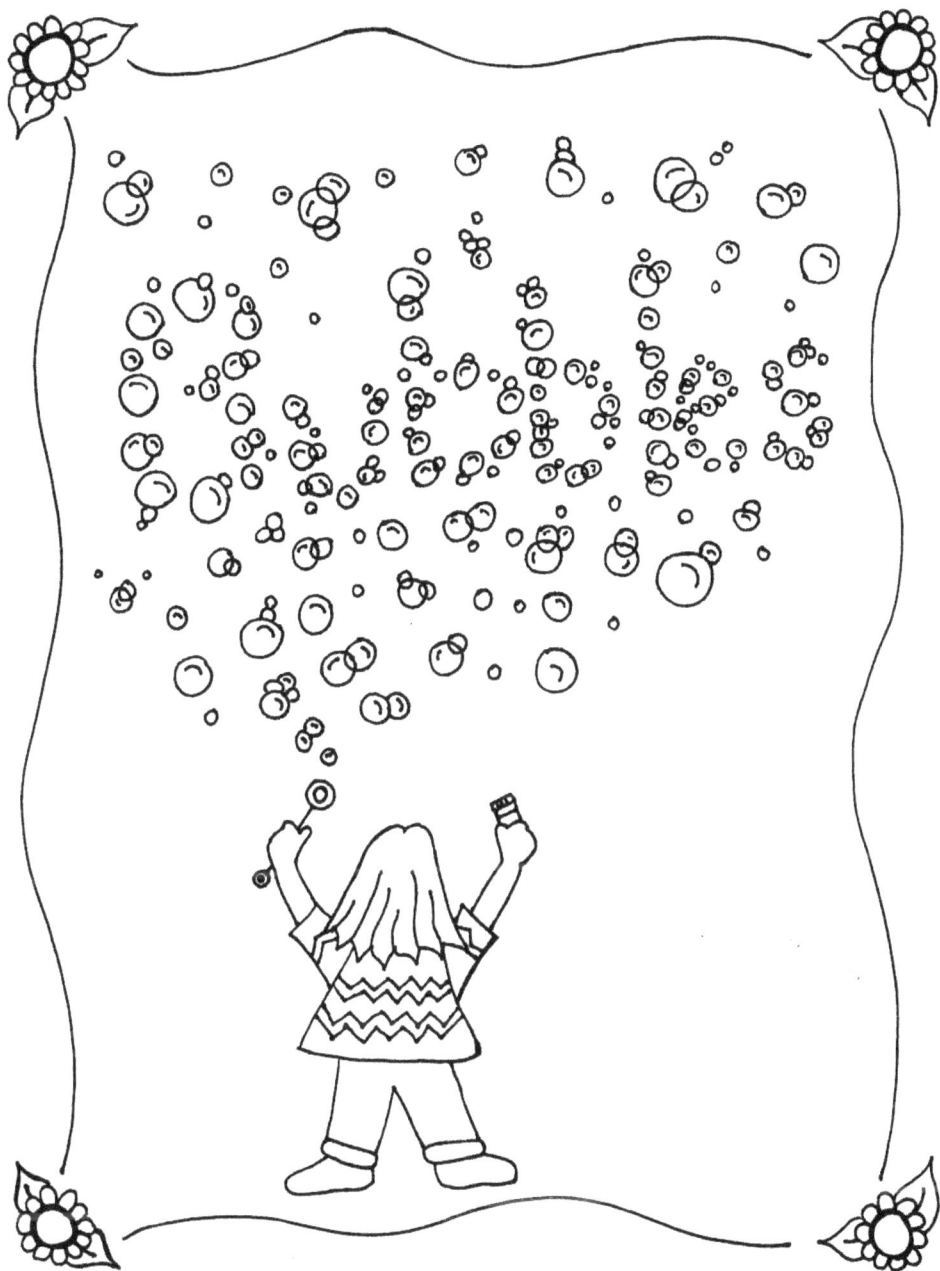

When I Am Scared, I Remember the

4 Safety BEES

1. BE Ready – Make a Safety Plan with an adult I trust

2. BE Calm - Take a deep breath and count to 10

3. BE Aware – Look around and find a safe space

4. **BE Supported** – Find an adult I trust to help me

I Have LOTS of
FEELINGS!

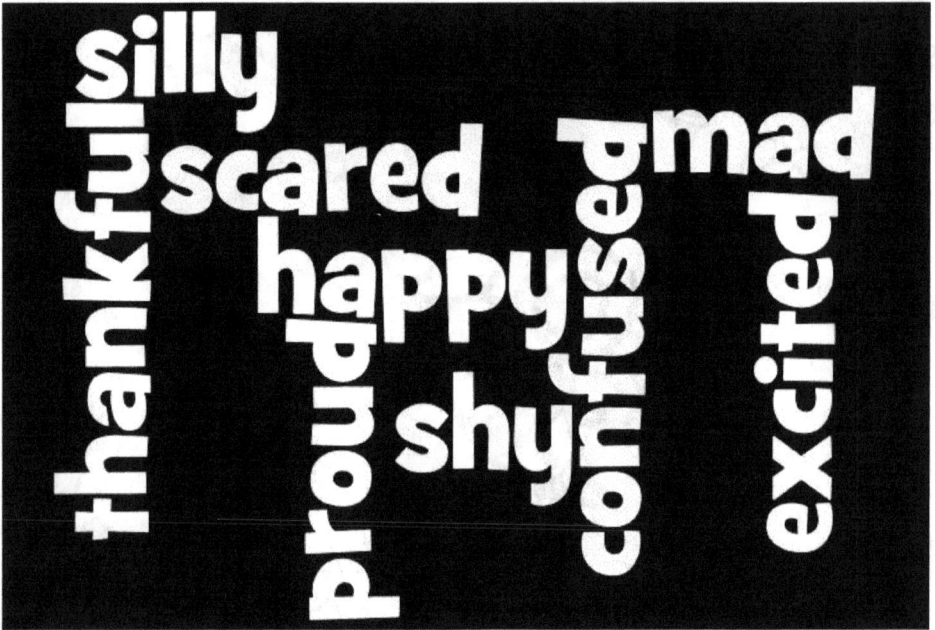

thankful silly scared happy proud shy confused mad excited

How Do I
FEEL TODAY?

Open My Eyes
What Do I See?

Wonderful Sights
All Around Me

Colors
Shapes
Happy Places

People Who Love Me

What Do My Eyes SEE
That Makes Me Feel
Calm & Safe?

SHHHHH...

Do You Hear What
I Hear?

Music & Singing
The Wind & The Rain

Soft Sounds
Loud Sounds

What Do I HEAR
That Makes Me Feel
Safe & Happy & Loved?

Soft

Fuzzy

Warm

Cozy

Cool

Smooth

Prickly

Bumpy

What Touches

My Hands & My Heart

And Gives Me

Hope?

HOPE

Mashed Potatoes,
Mac & Cheese

Chicken Nuggets,
Pizza Please

Blueberries, Apples,
Bananas, Too

If You Give Me Chocolate,

I'll Save Some for You!

Yummy Food Is Like a Hug

I Feel Safe & Snug!

My Favorite Food
Is:_____

When I Wiggle My Nose
And Take a Deep Breath,
What Will I Smell Today?

When the Smells Are Bad or
Scary or Weird
I Hold My Nose &
Count to 10!

Remember Happy Smells
Wiggle My Nose
And Then Breathe Again.

Ahhhhh, That's Better!

Close My Eyes

Breathe In

Breathe Out

Breathe In

Breathe Out

I'm Safe

I'm Calm

I'm Loved

Open My Eyes

Draw a Picture

of My Happy Place

Once Upon a Time …

I Was Born and I

GREW &

GREW &

GREW!

Tell Me a Story

My Story

The Story of the

One and Only ME!

Sometimes
My Feelings Get Stuck
In My Tummy
Or My Arms & Legs

My Body Says
Get UP & Move!

So I Play
I Run
I Dance

My Feelings Get Unstuck
I Feel Better

I Have a Little

LIGHT

Deep Down

Inside of ME

And When I Let It

Shine

It Always Helps Me to

SEE

Sometimes …
My Thoughts Get
JUMBLED

They Fly Around
TOO FAST in My Head

So I Breathe S-L-O-W-L-Y
I Look at These Buttons
I Color Them One-by-One

My Thoughts Slow Down
I'm Okay

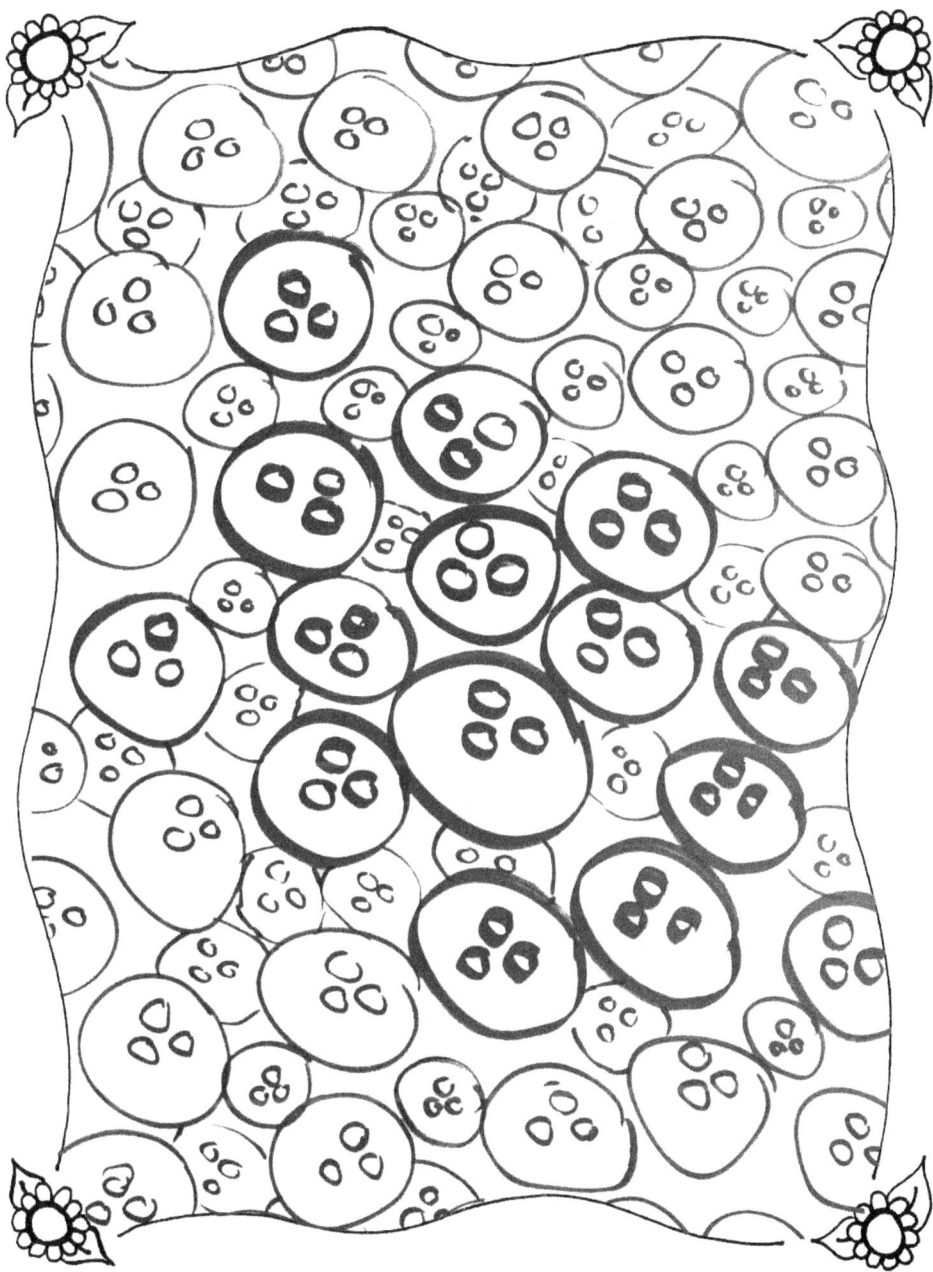

A GIRAFFE
Stands TALL
Above the Trees

He Is

BRAVE

I Can

Stand TALL &

Be BRAVE,
Too!

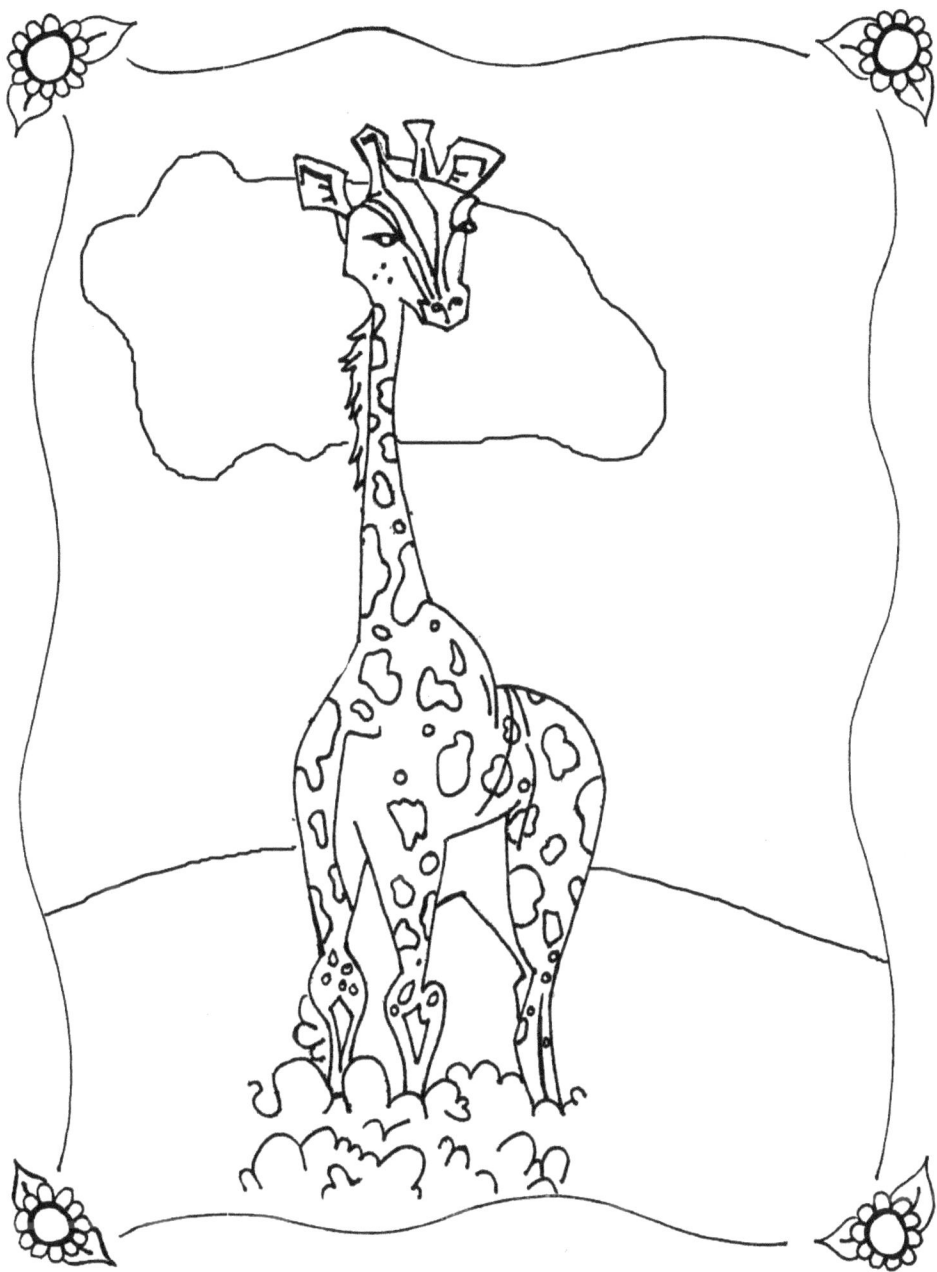

My FAMILY

Is like a

PUZZLE

We All
FIT TOGETHER
To Make a

Beautiful

Picture

of

Love!

When I Feel
Lonely or
Sad or
Scared

I Can Hug My
Teddy Bear
&
Remember
All the People
Who Love Me

I Can Do

LOTS of THINGS

But …

I Can't Drive a Car

Or Fly a Plane

(Not Yet … Someday)

So … for Now

I Am Happy There Are

BIG PEOPLE

To Help Me with the

BIG STUFF

I Close My Eyes

I Think

I Imagine

I Dream

When I Grow Up

I Want to Be …

I Open My Eyes

And I Draw

A Picture of My

DREAMS

When I Have a Boo-Boo
It Hurts

A Band-Aid

Makes It Better

Sometimes It Hurts
Inside my Heart

Bubbles & Music

Talking & Hugs

Are Like Band-Aids for
Inside of Me

The Rainbow Has Pretty Colors –
Blue, Green and Red and Orange.
After the Dark Rain Comes
A Bright Colorful Line in the Sky

That Rainbow Shows Me
Feelings of Beauty and Color
It Makes Me Feel Good Inside
It Makes Me Feel Like I Am Flying
in Blue Skylight
Rainbow Colors in My Eyes

Rainbows Are a
Good Part of My Day
When It Rains
There Will Always Be a Rainbow
Looking at Me
Saying Colorful Things to Me

The Rainbow Poem by Alysia Badeau

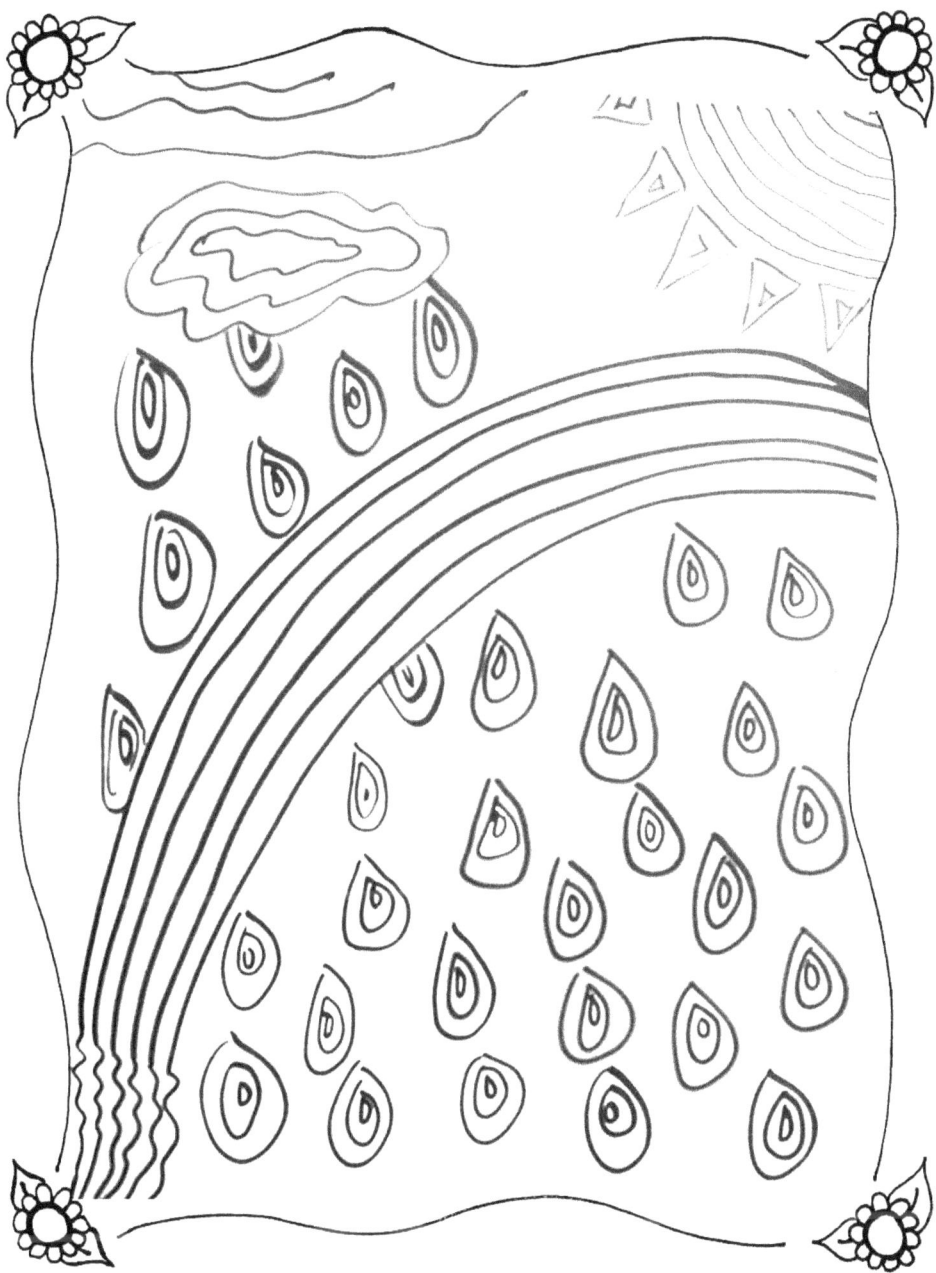

Wrenches &

Hammers & Nails

Are Tools for Building

Spatulas &

Spoons & Pots

Are Tools for Cooking

Coloring &

Talking & Dancing

Are Tools for

Feeling Better

When I Am

Sad, Mad or Scared

Little Flowers
Growing in the Bricks

You Are
Strong & Brave

Just Like ME!

I AM

STRONG

&

BRAVE,

Too

Additional Resources

A few key resources for further exploration are included on this page, and many more can be found in the companion, *"Building Bridges of Hope: A Coloring Book for Adults Caring for Children Who Have Experienced Trauma,"* also by Sue and Chelsea Badeau. You are encouraged to dig deeper using this list as a starting point. Consider it a scavenger hunt!

Experts

Juli Alvarado	Deborah D. Gray	Lisa Maynard	Jayne Schooler
Sandra Bloom	James Henry	Bruce Perry	Dan Siegel
Linda Burgess Chamberlain	Richard Kagan	Jolene Philo	Laurence Steinberg
Kenneth Ginsburg	Carol Kranowitz	Karen Purvis	Bessel van der Kolk

Websites about Childhood Trauma

Association for Training on Trauma and Attachment in Children: www.attach.org
Child Trauma Academy http://childtrauma.org
Harvard Center on the Developing Child http://bit.ly/1MtV1Dw and
http://bit.ly/1T4D39G
Multiplying Connections http://www.multiplyingconnections.org
NCTSN (National Child Traumatic Stress Network) www.nctsn.org
TCU Institute of Child Development http://child.tcu.edu

Activity Websites

Making Homemade Bubble Solution & Wands http://bit.ly/1VV68Xs
Coloring and Art Projects with Kids http://artprojectsforkids.org
Using Time-In, Not Time-Out, Purvis https://www.youtube.com/watch?v=T1-jOm2PyrA
Yoga and Guided Imagery with Kids http://www.cosmickids.com and
http://www.guidedimageryinc.com
"Roses and Thorns" Activity http://bit.ly/1SzDqWX

Books

1. Badeau, Hector, and Sue Badeau. *Are We There Yet? The Ultimate Road Trip: Adopting and Raising 22 Kids!* Franklin, TN: Carpenter's Son Publishing. 2013.

2. Gray, Deborah D. – Three books: *Nurturing Adoptions: Creating Resilience after Neglect and Trauma; Attaching through Love, Hugs and Play: Simple Strategies to Help Build Connections with Your Child* and *Games and Activities for Attaching with Your Child* (with Megan Clarke). London: Jessica Kingsley, 2012, 2014 and 2015.

3. Hughes, Daniel. *Attachment Focused Parenting: Effective Strategies to Care for Children* and other titles. W. W. Norton & Company. 2009.

4. Kagan, Richard. Real Life Heroes: *A Lifestory Book for Children* (3rd ed.) Abingdon, Oxon. Routledge. 2016.

5. Kranowitz, Carol. – Three books: *The Out-of-Sync Child. The Out-of-Sync Child Has Fun. The Out-of-Sync Child Grows Up.* Tarcher Perigee. 2006, 2006 and 2016.

6. Perry, Bruce Duncan, and Maia Szalavitz. *The Boy Who Was Raised as a Dog: And Other Stories from a Child Psychiatrist's Notebook: What Traumatized Children Can Teach Us about Loss, Love, and Healing*. New York: Basic, 2006.

7. Philo, Jolene. *Does My Child Have PTSD?: When Your Child Is Hurting from the inside out*.

8. Purvis, Karyn B., David R. Cross, and Wendy Lyons. Sunshine. *The Connected Child: Bring Hope and Healing to Your Adoptive Family*. New York: McGraw-Hill, 2007.

9. Wilgocki, Jennifer, Marcia Wright, Alissa Geis. *Maybe Days, A Book for Children in Foster Care.* Magination Press. 2002.

About the Author and Artists

Sue Badeau

The author, Sue Badeau, is a nationally known speaker, writer and consultant with a heart for children and families. After receiving a degree in Early Childhood Education from Smith College, Sue worked for many years in child services. Sue and her husband, Hector, are lifetime parents of 22 children, two by birth and 20 adopted. They have also served as foster parents and kin caregivers. They have authored a book about their family's parenting journey, *Are We There Yet: The Ultimate Road Trip, Adopting and Raising 22 Kids.* Sue may be reached at sue@suebadeau.com. Sue and Hector live in Philadelphia and are active in their community, Project HOME and Summit Presbyterian Church.

Chelsea Badeau

The principle artist and designer for this book is Chelsea Badeau. Chelsea is the director of editorial operations for a national media organization. She has an extensive background in creating and teaching art, including painting murals in the Philadelphia Family Courthouse and a church in Nanyuki, Kenya, as well as leading group painting sessions with her mom, Sue Badeau, on stress management techniques for caregivers of children who have experienced trauma. Chelsea graduated from Arcadia University and remains very active in her community. She lives with her two daughters in Philadelphia, spending many nights and weekends at sporting events with her children. Chelsea can be reached at chelsbadeau@aol.com.

Contributing Artists

Sue and Chelsea wish to offer great appreciation to the following contributors for adding to the uniqueness, diversity and richness of this book. **Alysia Badeau** contributed poetry (page 42) and the following guest artists added images for coloring. The titles and page numbers for their artwork is listed next to their names:

Abel Badeau –Heart-Hands (15), Teddy Bear (35), Toolbox (45)
Angel Vargas – Headphones (13), Comfort Foods (17),
Kandia Kovacs – Giraffe (31)
SueAnn Badeau Vargas – Candle (27), Buttons (29), Rainbow (43)

"Art is the stored honey of the human soul." Theodore Dreiser

www.ingramcontent.com/pod-product-compliance
Lightning Source LLC
Chambersburg PA
CBHW060643280326
41933CB00012B/2128